I0470925

Brains of birds..

Slumlords take our most of all.

Tricks to work are being hall.

Earth beguiles are charms to work.

Guns should chew and foods are worth.

Limbo ways are not so clear.

Speak with truths are gods to near.

Dirt for scales is life with dirt.

Cheat our gods are brains of birds.

---------Cheung Shun Sang=Cauchy3---------

Breads...

Bakery cakes have baking sheets.

Drive away your hunger needs.

Many kinds of breads are baked.

Cakes with cheeses are good and ate.

Blend the flour with milks as say.

Eat a dozen cakes for days.

Mixed with eggs are flours for cakes.

Nuts and fruits are season picks.

Dough can make in shapes are modes.

Dough with soda makes it go.

Go to baking sheets to bake.

Process cooking heats are takes.

------------Cheung Shun Sang=Cauchy3------------

Buds....

Brambles thrones are life are sad.

Hardships come and you might mad.

Berry sweets are smells that lead.

Life may flowers bed may sit.

Hills and clouds are up and down.

Season change as faces that found.

Fragrant things are lovely things.

Bees attracted and fragrant thick.

Dews will fill the life of buds.

Leaf and stem has roots and mud.

Stems protruded are flowers buds.

Flower charms are faces are marks.

Garden centre buy our seeds.

Flowers clusters scattered weeds.

Beauty weeds are rich as beds.

China tyranny...

China over lords beguiled you with all your claiming
futures. All their given benefits must have political
filters.

Laws are cruel all are not a birding.

Laws are dragnets all are birding nest and there are
loops with holes for open crotches that please the china
leaders tyrants dirty wills.

China tyrants seek us as leaders' fetishes.

Who can write the books of epochs must hush for
moneys also who can do accounts with cook accounts
for china lords.

Gullibility all are ways appeal to china peoples will that
may be tamed.

Those are china tyranny.

However those are secrets of real occurs as politics.

However those are rations of our gods to give that given
such with china politics.

What are gods to give by them as china tyrants leaders

Counter....

Wayward always are not for trust.

False to counter all are burst.

Counter claims are peoples' wishes.

Set it off recoiled are kisses.

Bullets kisses are tyrants' forces.

Some anti heroes just may loss.

Get recoiled are such reacts.

Some retorted are peoples' arts.

Tyrants' punches are evil arms.

China made the peoples harm.

In a jam are peoples' jams.

China tyrants get their games.

Bloody games have bloody hands.

Only vices are tyrants' lands.

Suffer well are peoples courses.

Critic one,...

Who as tyranny up to stages then we will cut their grounds from under.

Curtains fall and members all can leave.

Henchman and teacher pets are losses are missed..

China tyrants' sinful deeds can be a critic points.

China miffs and nursed wraths have piques for forces but would they win by tyrants also overlords forces.

Fingers in pies are wants are seeks for powers stuff as china commie teams or XI JINPING teams.

Get their apples pies to orders all as dictated signs.

Signs that high are they have means to all control for all of us.

Critic goes to antic home and spit or piss.

Just be guest and search our minds for good or wrong.

Just be guests and search our minds for bursts and putsch and files.

Know our stuffs are we the only men that obliged ways for saying yes.

,

Dreams that call..

Quackery says that something rigt have hidden meaning.

Dreams beside as something fulfill some ordinates

things many are sexual libido come so real and clear or

coming secretly.

There signs for sexual themes. A fig-a camera, a banana,

a choke, a dildo, a doll, a pig ,a dog, a tanks so as some

of them have tasks and means in dreams.

Psychic ways are feels and sense and thoughts and nerve

reflected.

Inner conflicts all are hidden themes that store to

dreams.

Neural paths are ways of brains.

Manifest contents all are ways may dream.

Dreams report from range so common also real or fancy

does as so special.

Some are wrong to say that dreams are window so

sacred.

Dreams could not be omen but latent sense that know

Fail..

Life has dirty chances.

Worship life or worship moneys get so shy.

Begging all are china laws are best regards for china tyrants tal

controls. One that seeks controls outside is tyrants' laws and

mores outsiders.

Real to make their moneys ranks may rim often.

Sells are Faust is worse than ever.,

Whole for global all may fear for dirt or no cheap dirt for beau

trades but all would like their dirty chances

Me as scandal monger also pimp of laws may write a lot for

justices.

Stick in eyes or beam in eyes are what had said.

China tyrants dip and flee as mouth on sticks will cheer me ip.

China tyrants nasty nice are plots are schemes are sins.

All to cross our globes as whole will worship moneys.

So please and come to fellate me if I am rich.

ERO by ways will sell their army weapon most for china tyrant

choices.

Hearts...

China anthems swear as TOURETTES syndrome.

China tyrants ME-ME-ME syndrome should there selfish
heads.

Full of touristy all are lands controlled. Not a bed of
roses is men to live so near to political cliffs.

Trap us all are eating stuffs that ate.

Bigger fishes are swim in smaller ponds.

Men as bigger girls with blouses are much.

China peoples' blow by blow accounts are needed.

Body songs are songs a cappella.

Yodel songs are loves and peace to keep.

China sirens songs come and come.

China tub thumping voices are siren songs.

Politic charms and baits have charm offense.

Tour de forces are bags of tricks that made infused to
take our all or cheat us some and give us funny counts.

There may always murders also bribery sins.

Money play a part on views of right and wrong so not as

Nights...

Nights are hallowed darks with dreams.

Sleeps are sleeps in pens with means.

Nightmare sounds are rattle snakes.

Venoms snakes will eat the pigs.

KAILYARDS green but mud is dirt.

Mice are bad and not a bird.

Birds are small and dreams are short.

Dreams may real but kingship not.

Dreams are kaizen works so swift.

Nights are weeps of gods that leave.

Night should sleep and not to play.

Dream a lot is days of hays.

Nights and days is biform in case.

Dreams about our meats have tastes.

Dreams in night may smooth and round.

Pass...

Roots and stems have pulling hard.

Moons and stars have climbed up marked.

Inner cycles have times that fast.

Spaces are wide and life would pass.

Birds are early all are wise.,

Tides will float as jumping lines.

All beyond our minds are guides.

Dreams may toss and run as dices.

Baptism life is life that fine.

Laws and life is sells and buys.

Life has files are bureau walls.

Walls for fires are not for all.

How and what is office rules.

Pass their times and snores are true.

Baffle gaps are heartless feels.

Peaks...

Laws certain and you may choke.

Collar me and books could cook.

Golden cuffs are moneys hush.

Laws abide and life could last.

Iceberg laws may need our heats.

Life may heat are human peaks.

Squadron needs the handle pans.

Foods are good and foods are friends.

Bursts on peaks are clocks with sync.

Catch our times are very things.

Pan for gold and all have ranks.

Men who peak can shake our hands.

Gold that peaked are shiny bright.

Men who rich have might for right.

Proper goose..

Proper goose is sexual acts.

Loves inspected the meats that add.

Take a gulp of cokes and gobble off.

Cupcake girls are south are north.

Likes to have are fuzz on fuzz.

Under roofs are loves to last.

More are better all are sexes.

Sexes exposed to honey pets.

Bang me gangs are very sexes.

Button joys are arts of heads.

Kiss your white bikini lines.

Costal paths have loves so fine.

LOTTA ways are sexes with modes

Stand for kisses are hard as nose.

Loves are running up as notches.

Sea...

Minds will go away from lakes or seas.

Marine forces are blasts are far or near.

Men excise arms at seas are forces.

Sea mistress will fight and get no loss.

Naval over lords will fight at best.

China evil dragons take no less.

Laws as customs all are ships at seas.

Heartfelt men will take our sign so near.

Wars disputed are men but storms are seas.

Grounds may swell so god must good to me.

Life details are seas and earth to pass.

Seas will look alike as clouds in masses.

-----------Cheung Shun Sang=Cauchy3----------

Sexes with modes...

Some desires of sexes are ices or fires.

Cool as winds are naughty things that shy.

Songs as horns are anthem ways as sexes.

Try for true is claim and begging facts.

Queens in queues are loves with sexes to lists.

Lusts of sexes are does to that as witches.

Quick and dirty all are cost for sexes.

Quickie sexes are not for lesbians checks.

Easy lay are names of tramps are cats.

Sexual ways are all explicated heads.

Goalie sexes will make her wishing much.

Chew and lick are soft nuts to touch.

Venus mounts are figs are much too much.

Scenes of sexes have blissful joys of lucks.

Joys of sexes are loving care not rants.

Tattoo..

Heart and sword is tattoo marks.

Mess your skins are beauty arts.

GOFFER fathers lotus come.

Chew your sugars chew your gums.

Funny farms have funny thoughts.

Notes are songs and years are chords.

Dagger cloaks are tattoo ways.

Laws are good and life is laid.

.

Tattoo things are arts that lay.

Bigger times have timer days.

Bosses are big and tattoo wise.

Share our turfs our friends are nice.

----------Cheung Shun Sang=Cauchy3---------------

Teach….

Teach by baffle gaps are fates.

Some disclaimers go with hates.

Feel ashamed are apples small.

Put to shame are tyrants all.

Daring masses are hero comes.

All may run so high and fun.

Up and surges are feels are ways.

Wretches have dirt that cheap to stay.

Bosses of laws are sullen men.

Landlord turfs have needs to pen.

Physic means are crimes are facts.

China tyrants' hearts have acts.

--------------Cheung Shun Sang=Cauchy3----------

Those are flowers...

All abundance comes to scenes.

Beauty flowers see as prints.

Steal our scenes are beauty one.

Flowers tunes are music tones.

Tulips cups are tall in stems.

Birds and buds are heaven teams.

Bright and fresh may smile in lights.

Beams and smiles are gods so right.

Florists' arts can speak to plants.

Plants and flowers those have sounds.

Speak to flowers all are nouns.

Flowers shrubs have books to count.

Garish those are clusters rounds.

Florists' minds are flower farms.

CARPELS good are pollens come.

Wars and wills...

Natural worlds will keep our minds.

Psyche things are freedom in.

Wills may free and loves may high.

Some believer laws so right.

Buying low are selling high.

Feel at spoons are bribe in signs.

Classic conflicts come for races.

Fetch with bloods are laws are traces.

Acts of wars are forms at ends.

Men may shake but laws may bend.

Bent to tyrants wills are ills.

Scribes in minds are something new.

China tyrants bent their laws.

Bend to favors all are all.

Tyrants favors all are cues.'

Wolves….

Some exact allusions all are bubbles ways.

Eager for all and grip and seize the all are life alike the bubble dreams.

Who will buy the worse and sell their souls that own in life. Hot and heavy feels of touches of serious life.

Dragons touches are evil touches are evil marks of china hosts or forces. Soldiers havoc cries are horns are drums are dangers.

Pardon Japan fishing island also set the Tibet free.

Indeed Tibet had be country own by self by Tibetans.

Points are good but laws might raw. China laws for universe are very bad.

Square deals are lines not arcs.

Circle rounds are cunning lines.

China inner circles all are eager going gets of careerism.

China jesters modes are china official common.

On the other side for British get the courts of common pleas that could take the place of human right with deals

Damned and treats are china ways...

Plato thoughts are upright logic also many ethics.

China says that each of us as china peoples must
appease them and they should obtain their godlike
ridden worlds as occurs and feels for their ways beside
their tyranny.

Plato feels no feel of sadist.

China tyrants do the sins.

However tyrants' indexes are ways that never somebody
come and hurt their feels otherwise all will damned and
treats.

Who have evil politic values just as rotten core?

However those as politic sadist shift by all excuse and
seek for bliss of feels.

Who have greatest ways as some esteems for all of self.

Pervert china cults had put other for commie shadows.

However pure as purest commie ways as those china do
are Saran also political sadist.

They some as all will seek for other trusts as dominated

Baggage...

China leftish guised as neutralism often tricks are nowadays.

They ask their peoples taking off epoch baggage much to welcome our china leftish some tyranny also most despotic.,

Faiths are baggage.

Traditions also much are baggage.

Laws abide are baggage.

Moral ways are baggage.,

Loves may also baggage come beside our pleasures.

It is my baggage.

It is heavy.

It is too heavy.

It is too heavy carrying them.

AM I CARRYING THEM?

British camber those are court or nation congress had been changed for several times in certain several ways.

Australia once at olden time had set up gathers called

Books to kiss..

Masters both of swords and pens.

Scribes are official reds are lens.

See from lens are worlds are bad.

China laws will create so mad.

Sole are words are tyrants pass.

Genteel men may come to ask.

Covered up faults are tyrants wish.

'Rich and bright are poems to kiss.

Styles of life are acts reached.

Bullets caps are firing caps.

Sing and dance beguile as truth.

Weep and sob are wail are turns.

Whether laugh or cries may not.

Jokes may bad and smiles are mocks.

Kisses have ranks and books can cook.

Bosom life..

Some require much are loves.

Great efforts are nothing half.

Waste our times are tyrants tricks.

Free our wills and life must wake.

Costing much are ways of life.

Cost us all are loves with might.

Proper ways will fight the vices.

Bosom friends would all so nice.

---------Cheung Shun Sang=Cauchy3-------------

www.ingramcontent.com/pod-product-compliance
Lightning Source LLC
Chambersburg PA
CBHW071604170526
45166CB00004B/1796